All Scripture references taken from the KJV of the Holy Bible, unless otherwise indicated.

Such & Such: *You Could Have Just Asked Me*
by Dr. Marlene Miles
Freshwater Press 2024
freshwaterpress9@gmail.com

ISBN: 978-1-965772-39-3

Paperback Version

Copyright 2024, Dr. Marlene Miles

All rights reserved. No part of this book may be reproduced, distributed, or transmitted by any means or in any means including photocopying, recording or other electronic or mechanical methods without prior written permission of the publisher except in the case of brief publications or critical reviews.

Table of Contents

Prayer 5
God Bless You 6
We Get Our Blessings from God 22
Prophet Nathan 26
David Needed Deliverance 32
Nathan the Prophet 35
Thy Master's House 38
The Master's Wives 43
Thrones of Israel and Judah 48
Is That Enough? 51
What *Else* Do You Want? 54
Ahithophel & Absalom 61
The Children of Ammon 64
The Sword Shall Not Depart 73
The Sins of the Ancestors 77
Is Satisfaction Possible? 81
Where Did Those Men Come From? 84
Me, Me, Me 91
Stones Into Bread? 97
What Shall I Do? 100
David Lost 106

Prayer Section 115

Dear Reader: 123

Prayerbooks by this author 124

Other books by this author 126

Such & Such

You Could Have Just Asked Me

Freshwater Press, USA

Prayer

Lord, bless the words of this book and open our hearts for hearing and understanding what the Spirit of the Lord is sharing and saying today, in the Name of Jesus. Lord, let Your Word ever make us new, improved and delivered. As we learn, let us not violate these principles that You hate us to violate, in the Name of Jesus. Amen.

God Bless You

Everyone wants to be blessed, but we must be very wise about how we get blessed and get blessings.

Does the Word of God say that what we want or feel that we want, or need is okay to **have**? Some things are not expedient for us to have. God knows best, what we should have and when. And why we should have it – what is its purpose in your life?

God provides all the things that we need but when it comes to what we **want**, then are we looking *elsewhere* for those *wanted* things? Where do we go for the things we want, although Psalm 23 says we should not *want*? We should not yearn, or lust for anything. We know that the lust for money is the root of all evil, although in and of itself money may not be bad to have, to use or to help. But lust is always bad.

God may not have approved for those *wanted* things to come into our lives yet, but if we move from desire to want, to lust, we put ourselves in harm's way. God's choices for us protect us; we should obey God when it comes to things we acquire in life.

This requires a proper relationship with God. It requires constant communication with God. This book is more about getting things we want than gaining or regaining things that have been taken from us.

So, if it's taking a minute to get something we want from God, Is God perfecting some matter in us making us ready and right so when we get that thing, or those things, we don't turn into a prideful egomaniac, or worse? Sometimes the delay is that God is protecting us from ourselves, keeping us from becoming puffed up, or no Earthly good because of being blessed or over-blessed.

Is God preparing us so when we get that thing, we can KEEP that thing once we receive it?

In the Old Testament Abraham went off to war against 5 kings, and this is when he first began to get really rich. God was teaching Abraham and just as God teaches our hands for battle and our fingers to fight.

The same power, prowess and skills that it takes to get a thing will be used to KEEP that thing, because doesn't the loser always want a rematch? Doesn't the loser want the best two out of three? The loser wants to come back; the loser wants to retaliate; the loser wants a rematch. You have to defend the blessings that the Lord has put in your hands. Amen.

Those who are foraging for blessings must not be in Christ, because God provides all things to His children. God is not a deadbeat Dad. Many who are foraging are going from religion to religion, trying to pick the goodies off each table.

God is not about that.

Can your husband do that? Can he go from house to house and get the *goodies* of that house and then come home to you and still be your husband?

Then why do you think you can do it?

Can your wife do that? Can she get what she wants or feels she needs from other men, and then come home to you and still be your wife?

God hates this – it is adultery. It is spiritual adultery when you do it regarding spiritual matters. It is idolatry.

So, what do you really believe in? Who do you believe in? Everything and everyone cannot be the answer, although many throughout the world worship many deities. God is not about that; it is not God's way.

Hear, O Israel: **The Lord our God is one Lord:** (Deuteronomy 6:4)

God blesses His people with good things. In the Old Testament, gleaning was for the poor. It was customary to leave a portion of the harvest in the field for the poor. God blesses His people; He does not make us glean and look for our own blessings as if we are on a scavenger hunt.

In Scandinavian countries they observe something called, All Men's Right. It allows you to roam in any wood, meadow or field to forage for wild food. As long as you don't cut down trees or break twigs, the owner of the land can't stop you or ask for compensation.

It's not like that here in this country, but yes, people will leave a little for the poor. The saved and those with good consciences give of their substance to others, through ministries and directly to charities. We presume the poor are usually the unsaved, but the widow and the oppressed may receive from one another ministry, as well.

God rains on the just and the unjust alike, and it is the intention of the saved, as they minister food and other needs to the unsaved that they will draw the unsaved to Christ. The goal is usually evangelism, to draw the sinner or backslidden to Christ so that they enter into relationship with Him, or re-enter into relationship with the Lord God if they've been backslidden.

The purpose of giving to the underprivileged is not that they get to glean or forage forever, because that is living far below the level that God planned for His people to live their lives.

Until the Word is preached to them, the forager may believe that this is the way it is. The forager might want to go out and seek what he or she *wants* rather than to be in the House of God, knowing that what they earnestly seek and ask God for will come to them if they are in Christ.

Why?

Because the uncommitted can just get the goodies and leave the rest. They may believe that they can hit it and quit it. You can get it and be gone. The places where you are foraging from require nothing of you – *so you think.*

However, that is not so. There is always a spiritual price to pay for whatever you get.

Would you rather be in relationship with Jehovah Jireh, who provides all your needs according to His riches in glory, providing all things for your life and godliness and you know what is required of you, OR would you rather forage for blessings, here and there and everywhere–, thinking that you are getting over and getting *by*?

For such a person, the motivation might be because you don't want to follow the Bible, read the Bible or give offerings in a church, or deal with those church people. That is a very anti-Christ attitude. Still, you will end up owing spiritual debt because of what you got from entities that are **NOT GOD,** ***not* Jehovah God.**

Would you rather owe 100 lesser *gods* –(which are really demons and devils, trying to impersonate GOD)? Most unsaved people may not believe there is a God, or any *gods* so the food offerings they may have received, for example, is theirs for the taking. They believe that they deserve it. If they owe anyone, it is the person who gave that to them, or the agency behind that person. But it was a gift, so they feel that they don't owe anyone anything, even if they could afford to pay. They also may not be thinking spiritually, they are just walking by sight.

It's not so simple; there is spiritual debt. If you didn't get it from God, now you owe idol *gods* things that you don't even know what you owe, and things you can't pay, so now your life becomes miserable, devastated, robbed and you can never pay them back anyway, so now these *spiritual* penalties and requirements go to your generations.

What?

Like a good parent who may ask the child who shoplifted the candy from the corner store, "Why didn't you tell me you wanted candy? I would have gotten it for you."

- Why didn't you tell me you were hungry? I would have given you food to eat?
- You didn't have to forage: Jehovah Jireh is our provider.
- You didn't have to beg.
- You didn't have to go out into the streets and hustle that way.
- You didn't have to steal.
- You didn't have to make devil deals at all. Most of all you didn't have to make dark deals that would put you and your family on the hook with the devil for generations.

GOD will provide all things for life and for godliness. Idol *gods* provide dark things, evil things. Idols give power to a person who should not have power. For a price. Fame to the ambitious person who is lusting for it. For a price. Money--, crazy money to the person who will sell their own soul. It is not money for money; it is a soul for money. One thing about that is if a man will sell his **own** soul, then selling the soul of another is no big thing to him.

But God provides. God **gives**. He gives with no strings attached, no sorrow with what God gives us. God loves. Love gives. The only requirement is RELATIONSHIP. What is your relationship with God.

The devil has no love and he doesn't give; he sells and steals and kills and destroys. He makes transactions he doesn't give.

God so loved the world and God loves, so He blesses and gives. The requirements for relationship with god are in the Bible, but there may be specific things that you need to do to work out STUFF that is only in you, such as pride, greed, selfishness – *you know. Most often what you have to work out to enter into the Kingdom of Heaven is the very thing you don't want to let go of.* Demonic *spirits* hide, or they make you believe that they are not there, or that they are not what they are. *Pride* may have you believing that you have excellence, calling yourself a perfectionist. It could be *pride*. Sorry.

Greed may have you thinking that you are behind, and you never get what others get and it's really not fair. So, *greed* may masquerade as assertiveness convincing you that you've been passive all your life and that's why you've been looked over, stepped over, or stepped on. Yup.

Selfishness, for example, may have you believing that you are just looking out for yourself because no one else will, calling it self-preservation. Uh huh. So, believing all these lies, all these lying demons you embrace pride, and greed, and selfishness all the more. Why in the world would you want to get rid of such helpful feelings and attitudes?

Because they are not helpful. They are not Godly, and they are lying to you, keeping you bound and not blessed because you haven't met the *requirements*. God is not going to bless these demons. A man with these attitudes, has the corresponding demons. God is not blessing that.

So, you have to get rid of attitudes and traits, characteristics that are not conducive to you receiving from the Lord. But you can receive; you don't need to go out and beg or glean, or forage for blessings from other *gods*, when Jehovah is waiting to bless you.

In relationship, the Lord will not leave you to suffer and do without. Neither will He make you have to SIN to get any good thing. But the criteria is that you present yourself as a whole soul to the Lord, not encumbered with a bunch of demonic *spirits*--, they can't hide in you as not to be seen by God. They can't fool the Lord. He knows when you need deliverance and will often require it to protect you from taking on the nature of the demons and then begin to sin.

Deliverance before you sin, is so you don't sin, and so He can bless you. With evil *spirits* on board, even those that are hidden to you, and in masquerade, it is only a matter of time before a man sins. The goal of those *spirits* is to make a man sin, so they can stay and create more problems for this man's life.

David defeated Goliath. David worshipped the Lord in Spirit and in Truth. David was a man after God's own heart and in their relationship, God blessed David mightily. Saints of God, the only gifts you want are from the Lord, trust that.

And I gave thee thy master's house, and thy master's wives into thy bosom, and gave thee the house of Israel and of Judah; and if *that had been* too little, I would moreover have given unto thee **such and such** things. (2 Samuel 12:8, emphasis added, mine)

Whereby are given unto us exceeding great and precious promises: that by these ye might be partakers of the divine nature, having escaped the corruption that is in the world through lust. 2 Peter 1:4

When you get and accept gifts from unknown and evil sources this is when corruption enters. This is when you have entered the Dark Kingdom instead of the Kingdom of Heaven, God's Kingdom, the Kingdom of light.

In the dark kingdom, there is corruption, which is: depravity; wickedness; perversion or deterioration of moral principles; loss of purity or integrity. And, corruption leads to death.

The wages of sin is death. Along with sin comes the *iniquity* of that sin and the Curse of the Law.

We Get Our Blessings from God

David killed a lion and a bear and then he faced Goliath. First, the lion, and then the bear, then bigger opponents came to David. It should be true of us as well, as the Lord is teaching our hands to war and our fingers to fight.

Then at another time of war, David had become king, both over Judah and all of Israel--, both kingdoms. Everyone else was at war, but not David. He was rooftop gazing, and it was then and there that he spotted Bathsheba.

You all know the story. David eyed Bathsheba. He sent for her; he impregnated her--, another man's wife.

David killed a lion, a bear, and a giant, but *lust* defeated him that day.

Then David tried to cover up his sin, but that didn't work. Next, he basically had Bathsheba's husband made unalive by sending Uriah back into the war.

Then David marries Bathsheba after Uriah's' death, but he is still nose blind to the fact that he did anything wrong. Well, he's king, after all, can't he do as he pleases?

David may have realized within himself that he was wrong, but he may have been thinking that no one else knew, or no one else outside of the palace knew what he had done, and he most likely wanted to protect his reputation with his *subjects*.

Saints of God when do we think we have *arrived* as kings? When we get everything that we *want* from God? Is that when we feel we are higher than our neighbors? Is that when we believe we can become lawless? Higher than other people? Is that when we become king, so now we can do whatever we want?

Those attitudes are the things that need to be worked out in us. Before we receive mightily from God. Else that could be why a lot of us don't receive.

David doesn't just *think* he is king, he really **is** king. Does that mean he can do whatever he wants to do? Well, folks, a lot of kings have gotten into major trouble with God – so your title and your situation and your station don't matter – right is right and wrong is wrong.

He suffered no man to do them wrong: yea, he **reproved kings for their sakes;**. Saying, Touch not mine anointed, and do my prophets no harm. (Psalm 105:14-15)

God isn't playing with any of us. He said that He would reprove kings for our sake. He was not pleased with Saul, Ahab was known as about the worst king of all, God and Pharoah got into it. Joash, Herod, Amaziah, Josiah and Nebuchadnezzar, to name some other kings that God had to deal with, in no particular order.

Back to this story: Uriah is **DEAD**. Because David committed sexual sin and then by impregnating Bathsheba, David has interfered in a **marriage covenant**. Now that Uriah is dead, David has essentially terminated Bathsheba's and Uriah's *'til death do us part* marriage covenant as well as terminating Uriah.

Uriah's death was **untimely** because David manipulated it.

Prophet Nathan

God sends Nathan the prophet – saints of God have you noticed that kings are assigned prophets all throughout the Bible so the voice of God can be heard by these kings who may become absolutely corrupt – because many of them did. In our modern times, many people still become corrupt; they get drunk with power. David was among them in this Bathsheba Gate, the Bathsheba scandal.

So, Nathan tells David the story of the rich man who had plenty of sheep, but he wanted the one ewe lamb of a poor man. When he heard this story, David was livid, until Nathan the

Prophet said to David, "And that man is you."

And the Lord sent Nathan unto David. And he came unto him, and said unto him, There were two men in one city; the one rich, and the other poor.

The rich man had exceeding many flocks and herds:

But the poor man had nothing, save one little ewe lamb, which he had bought and nourished up: and it grew up together with him, and with his children; it did eat of his own meat, and drank of his own cup, and lay in his bosom, and was unto him as a daughter.

That one ewe lamb was as a pet to the poor man. (Mercy Lord, the rich man is *eating the pets* from the poor man's farm*!)*

And there came a traveller unto the rich man, and he spared to take of his own flock and of his own herd, to dress for the wayfaring man that was come unto him; but took the poor man's lamb, and dressed it for the man that was come to him.

And David's anger was greatly kindled against the man; and he said to Nathan, As the Lord liveth, the man that hath done this thing shall surely die:

And he shall restore the lamb fourfold, because he did this thing, and because he had no pity.

And Nathan said to David, Thou art the man. (2Samuel 12:1-7)

Oh, there's more:

And Nathan said to David, Thou art the man. Thus saith the Lord God of Israel, I anointed thee king over Israel, and I delivered thee out of the hand of Saul;

And I gave thee thy master's house, and thy master's wives into thy bosom, and gave thee the house of Israel and of Judah; and if that had been too little,

I would moreover have given unto thee *such and such* things.

Wherefore hast thou despised the commandment of the Lord, to do evil in his sight? thou hast killed Uriah the Hittite with the sword, and hast taken his wife to be thy wife, and hast slain him with the sword of the children of Ammon.

Now therefore the sword shall never depart from thine house; because thou hast despised me, and hast taken the wife of Uriah the Hittite to be thy wife.

Thus saith the Lord, Behold, I will raise up evil against thee out of thine own house, and I will take thy wives before thine eyes, and give them unto thy neighbour, and he shall lie with thy wives in the sight of this sun.

For thou didst it secretly: but I will do this thing before all Israel, and before the sun.

And David said unto Nathan, I have sinned against the Lord. And Nathan said unto David, The Lord also hath put away thy sin; thou shalt not die.

> Howbeit, because by this deed thou hast given great occasion to the enemies of the Lord to blaspheme, the child also that is born unto thee shall surely die.
>
> And Nathan departed unto his house. And the Lord struck the child that Uriah's wife bare unto David, and it was very sick. (2 Samuel 12:10-15)

I love that passage in the New Testament when Jesus said that the prince of this world cometh, but he has nothing in him (John 14:30). That meant that Jesus was above reproach, sin free, and couldn't be touched.

David, not so much. Verse 14, the Lord says that because of what David has done, the enemy now has been given an opportunity to speak evil against mankind in general, and against King David in particular. Remember the devil is the Accuser, standing before God night and day to accuse the brethren. David, you just gave the devil so much to talk about, and now I've got to listen to that, is what I imagine the Lord's implication to be.

David Needed Deliverance

How could David possibly need deliverance when God had *delivered* him already?

And Nathan said to David, Thou art the man. Thus saith the Lord God of Israel, I anointed thee king over Israel, and I delivered thee out of the hand of Saul;

The Lord God had delivered David from the hand of Saul. As you recall, Saul wanted to kill David; God spared David's life. Part of Saul's problem with David was that the Prophet Samuel had many years prior already anointed David to be king. Saul was jealous of David. Saul was disobedient to God and had been rejected as king.

God delivered David out of the murderous plans of Saul. God delivered David, physically out of harm's way into safety.

David needed deliverance; he still needed to be delivered spiritually. No, God didn't miss it, David did. As is common to man, being king will many times go to a man's head. God had tried to talk the people out of demanding for a king when at the time they had judges. But the people insisted. Think back a bit further when the people demanded an idol while Moses was upon Mount Sinai meeting with God and getting the Ten Commandments. Collectively, or individually, if you want to learn your lessons the easy way, by listening to and obeying God, then do it that way. If you want to learn your lessons the hard way, well sometimes God will just let you do it that way.

Don't you imagine that sometimes God is just shaking His holy head?

Folks, by the time a real prophet anoints you as king, that is some serious grace on you. Shouldn't a man then at least try to conduct himself with dignity and in a manner befitting his new station in life?

After getting saved, people still need deliverance.

David proved that after getting anointed, deliverance is still the children's bread; and deliverance is still necessary--, even for kings.

Nathan the Prophet

Nathan came with the Word of God. The Word of God, with a man's repentance will effect deliverance. The Word of God, along with the infant getting sick is when David began to fast and repent. He still had iniquity to pay, however, therefore the child ended up dying. The wages of sin is death. Something died, someone died – not either of the two sinners, but their offspring –, a son: David's strength. The male infant died.

> And David said unto Nathan, I have sinned against the Lord. (2 Samuel 12:13a)

David acknowledged his sin very quickly once the Word of the Lord was presented to him. We know that David did a lot of repenting, especially in the Psalms. We know that David was serious and sincere, not just giving lip service to Nathan. We know this because David contemplated on his sin and his repentance and even wrote down this and other Psalms, or at least had them to be written down. That is an official act of a king to have something recorded for posterity.

David owned this sin.

Have mercy upon me, O God, according to thy lovingkindness: according unto the multitude of thy tender mercies blot out my transgressions.

Wash me thoroughly from mine iniquity, and cleanse me from my sin.

For I acknowledge my transgressions: and my sin is ever before me.

Against thee, thee only, have I sinned, and done this evil in thy sight: that thou mightest be justified when thou speakest, and be clear when thou judgest. (Psalm 51:1-4)

We serve a God with largeness of heart and great Mercy. He will not refuse a broken heart or a contrite spirit.

The sacrifices of God are a broken spirit: a broken and a contrite heart, O God, thou wilt not despise. (Psalm 51:17)

And Nathan said unto David, The Lord also hath put away thy sin; thou shalt not die. (2 Samuel 12:13b)

The wages of sin is death. But God forgave David and Bathsheba; they didn't die, but their child did.

Thy Master's House

In the Word of the Lord through Nathan the Prophet to David the King says:

And I gave thee thy masters house, thy masters wives into thy bosom, and gave thee the House of Israel and Judah. And if that had been too little. I moreover, would have given unto thee such and such things.(2 Samuel 12:8)

The master's house is the house you used to work in. Remember David used to work for Saul; he was the minstrel for King Saul, he was placed there to cheer Saul in the palace because Saul was king then, but now David is king. (10 years after being anointed). God is saying, I gave thee thy master's house and now you have people working for you; now you are king. God has given him many exceeding great and precious promises. And he would have given him **Such and Such** promises if David had asked.

Just ask.

Don't you hate it when people take something from you when they just could have asked you? and you would have given it to them.

God is speaking to David and God just wants you, in faith to ask Him , ask Him for the things that we want. The things we *really* want. God will give us the desires of our hearts. God must hate it when mankind goes to the dark kingdom to do evil, bypass God and do evil things.

Now you own that house. Now you have people working for you. Your relationship with God so tight that you can ask Him for anything, even SUCH & SUCH things. All you have to do is ask Him.

God just wants you to ask Him. In faith, we are to ask God for the things we want—the things we *really* want. He has said He will give us the desires of our heart. What does that mean to you? For King David it was a number of things, and God was faithful to bless him abundantly. God gave David at least four things for slaying Goliath. Truthfully before David went out to meet Goliath, he had asked God, "What's in it for me?" David showed us his worldliness by even asking that.

What David got for slaying Goliath was huge. He got to marry King Saul's daughter, Michal. He and his family became exempt from paying taxes, forever. To me that means that working for God, especially going to get God's stuff back, or protecting God's people as

David did when he slew Goliath, working for God pays very well. It pays as well or better than any other kind of work you can think of doing because of the spiritual benefits that even outweigh the natural pay and rewards.

God gave King David his master's house. The house you used to *serve* in means that God has reversed your slavery, turned your captivity, changed your servanthood so now you are the head, and not the tail. God has reversed your bondage, setting you free. That is just like God.

If that weren't enough, He turns around and gives you the mansion on the hill, that house that you used to *admire* when you were a kid. The house you used to drive by when you were a student. And you may have even worked there, polishing the fittings and furnishings, cleaning the windows, or planting gardens, mowing the lawn, taking care of that house as though it were yours, diligently. Diligence has it's own rewards.

Now here it is. He just gave it to you,

And if ye have not been faithful in that which is another man's, who shall give you that which is your own? (Luke 16:12).

David used to serve in a palace, now he lives in a palace. Now it is your turn to live in the nice house, saints of God. Thank the Lord when He has delivered and turned your captivity.

The Master's Wives

God told David he had given him his **master's wives**. In those days when you conquered a king, a village or a nation, you took the women –, you took the children too, but you took the women. that meant you had conquered them for sure, because you took their women.

If you take this literally then your master's wives are those women who are just too hot for you as you are, or as you were, but when God blows you up, then you attract all the beautiful people who used to be afar off from you--, out of your league.

Your master's wives: That means *intimate things*. God has given you as a prize for your obedience, discipline, service, and because of your relationship with Him--, your master's wives. If you're a man or a woman, it doesn't matter, these wives represent God having given you **people** to minister to you, people to minister to your needs. Wives are known as helpmates, destiny helpers. God has provided destiny helpers for you.

Just as you have served, prayerfully, diligently, you now shall *be* served. He has put **people** in your path to assist you in accomplishing things you need to get done in your life.

You now have divine favor when you go places. People go out of their way to assist you and to help you succeed. That's God. The favor of God is on your life. When the favor of God is on you, man will also favor you.

Not only that, but you will also humiliate your former captor by having what your captor had as yours. If what you are getting back from an enemy, for example, is something that they took from you, then they have to repay sevenfold. This restitution the enemy must make to you may be in money, tangible goods, or even his servants, or his women. Even the master's wives.

If it is spoils of war, then there is no limit to what all you may win, as long as that war was sanctioned by God. If it was, then God surely helped you win and gave you the victory.

But Uriah was not an opponent of David; Uriah was not an enemy of David. David had no reason to conquer Uriah by taking the man's wife, other than David, because of the demons in his soul made Uriah into an enemy and unjustifiably so. Bathsheba was not a spoil of war because David wasn't at war with Uriah, at least he wasn't supposed to be at war with friends. Uriah was his brother, in the spirit of the Lord.

When defeating a real enemy, spoils, such as the women, God gives them to the victor. All that the enemy used against you, the enemy's things, his prized possessions have now become as spoils of war. You have just earned all manner of valuable things from warfare, from your obedience and walking upright before the Lord. as God declares you victor of the battles.

God did not declare David victor over Uriah.

All that the enemy used against you, all that he flaunted in your face, is now yours to use with wise spiritual discretion. That is why God had to change you so you wouldn't go overboard when you finally got it; He had to change your character. God has released you from captivity and bondage. Some of your captivity and bondage were the evil spirits that caused you to take on their nature, such as *greed, pride*, and *lust*. But now you're delivered, right? Now God has endowed you with these great blessings.

Thrones of Israel and Judah

Fear not, little flock; for it is your Father's good pleasure to give you the kingdom. (Luke 12:23)

It is the Father's good pleasure to give you the Kingdom, and that is far more valuable than the key to the city. But you want that key? You don't have to steal it. Ask God, He will give you your heart's desire, even **Such & Such**. Pray that the Lord ill grant you into the Kingdom, and that all the people will be willing when the Lord exalts you.

God further said to David that He gave him the thrones of Israel and Judah. What could that possibly mean to us? These Thrones represent heavenly and earthly power. With great benevolence

God shows you divine favor and gives you **authority, position,** and **power.** He sets you in dominion. He gives you, me, all of us the *Thrones of Israel and Judah.*

How so?

And I gave thee thy master's house, and thy master's wives into thy bosom, and gave thee the house of Israel and of Judah; and if that had been too little, I would moreover have given unto thee *Such and Such things.* (2 Samuel 12:8)

If that had been too little --- all the blessings of God are exceedingly more than we could ever ask or think. They are perfect, coming down from the Father of Heavenly Lights.

Yet God says to David, if that had been too little... I would moreover have given you Such & Such things.

For all the promises of God in him are yea, and in him Amen, unto the glory of God by us. Now he which stablisheth us with you in Christ, and hath anointed us, is God; (2 Corinthians 1:20-21)

Is That Enough?

Christ, who is in the lineage of David and of the Tribe of Judah, sits on the Throne of heavenly power. We are in Christ. We are created for good works, crowned with Glory & Honor, set on high to have dominion, God is blessing us with all things for life and godliness. Being seated with Christ in a place of high authority is spiritual power; it is a throne of power.

Is that enough? Is there something more that you want?

You don't need to forage for blessings. You don't need to go to the dark side to get anything.

Is that enough is what the Lord wants to know.

If not, ask Him and He will give you all things, all things, all things.

If that had been too little – GOD was asking David and anyone with ears to hear, why did you wander off to get things that I would have given you, if you had just asked?

- Why did you ask a foreign power for what I would have given you?
- Why did you ask an idol *god*, a devil, or a demon?

Jesus, in His Wilderness temptations, didn't take from the devil because God supplies everything that He would ever need or want – even into abundance.

Jesus is seated at the right hand of Glory in spiritual authority over all things that the Father created. The Throne of Israel upon which David sat represented that spiritual authority; those things pertain to our godliness.

For the things that pertain to our life, the other tribes, which comprised the balance of the people of God, represent Earthly power. God is giving you all these things that pertain to life and godliness. He's giving you all the things you need to be in power and authority in Earthly *and* Heavenly realms.

Is there anything else? Is there something else that you want?

If so, then ask God for it. Sit and reason with the Lord, and ask for what you want.

What *Else* Do You Want?

Think of the vastness of God. Think of how God is infinite; what else do you want? Think of the awesomeness of God, then ponder, if you must, why He asked David and why He might be asking you: *"What else do you want?"*

His Word says, if you abide in Me and My Word abide in you, you shall ask what you will, and it shall be given – it shall be done for you. Even **Such & Such**, saints of God.

Is there a Godly purpose to what you want? Then it is an *abiding* request. These may be reasons why God is asking you. Consider the following:

- There's more for you than all that He has already given you; He is El Shaddai, the God of More than Enough. God is infinite.
- He wants you to have *more* than just what you got. He gives more than you could ever ask or think.
- God wants to know if you're satisfied. Of course, if you voluntarily went back and thanked Him, and praised Him, He would know your heart on what you have received and what He has done for you. Should God even have to ask you to say, *Thank You?*
- God wants to know, *can you be* satisfied.

This gets deep because it is the flesh that cannot be satisfied--, well, permanently satisfied. We are satisfied after today's meal, but we will be hungry again.

> Who satisfieth thy mouth with good things; so that thy youth is renewed like the eagle's. (Psalms 103:5)

Asking if you are satisfied is God's gauge on who you are right now. Really, He already knows, so it is God who is asking you to look at yourself and do a self-assessment. Are you satisfied? Can you be satisfied. If not, why?

> Three things that never say it is enough: The horseleach hath two daughters, crying, Give, give. There are three things that are never satisfied, yea, four things say not, It is enough:
>
> The grave; and the barren womb; the earth that is not filled with water; and the fire that saith not, It is enough. (Proverbs 30:15-16)

God wants us satisfied. He even says in Psalm 91 that we can live until we are satisfied. By the time you get to Glory when it is all said and done, God doesn't want you soul tied to the Earth, because you didn't finish everything you wanted to complete. God doesn't want you soul tied to the cucumbers, garlic and leeks. God expects all of us to get on with life and live until we are satisfied. As humans, that should be easy to do since God is assisting us all the way.

With long life I will satisfy him and show him my salvation.(Psalm 91:16)

If God would go through the trouble of asking you, ***What else do you want?*** Then you should be honored to serve such a God. He's telling you that He would have given you ***such and such*** if you had asked Him. It's scriptural, ***such and such*** is in the Bible, And that's a whole lot of stuff. ***Such and Such*** encompasses everything you can think of and everything that your heart desires.

The things that we ask God for, that we think are such big things, are really little things to God. As long as we abide in Him, God says that whatever we ask for, He will give it to us. Jesus says if we ask the Father in His name, He will give it to us that the Father may be glorified in the Son.

If ye abide in me, and my words abide in you, ye shall ask what ye will, and it shall be done unto you. (John 15:7)

But this is where that *abiding* comes into play: especially with David, but think of your case.

- How are you going to ask God for another man's wife?
- How are you going to ask God to break another's marriage covenant when we know that God hates broken Godly covenant.
- How are you going to ask God to let you fornicate or commit adultery and then give the person back to their spouse? That's what David was trying to do, *hit it and*

quit it. David paid a heavy spiritual price for that plan.
- How can Bathsheba be over at the palace with David and then come back home and still be Uriah's wife?
- How are you going to let your own child be raised by another man, turning your back on your own flesh and blood? God is our Father. Everything He does toward us is fatherly. He does not expect that some other entity would step in to do anything at all for us, especially masquerading as helper or a mother or a father, or as our God.
- David was planning to let another man claim and raise David's child. Is that not child sacrifice?
- How can any of us, in good conscience try to get all the good from God that we can and then go into the dark kingdom to get evil

things and accomplish wickedness?
- How can any of us that do that and then think that God doesn't know, and we are still right in step with God as we were the last time we were walking upright before Him.

Thank God for repentance and His great Mercy, so we can come back home if we repent. We must decide if we are God's child or Satan's.

Ahithophel & Absalom

Seek wise counsel, people of God. I kinda suspect that Ahithophel wasn't satisfied and could not be satisfied, else he wouldn't have advised David the way that he did.

> And Ahithophel said to Absalom, "Go in to your father's concubines, whom he has left to keep the house; and all Israel will hear that you are abhorred by your father. Then the hands of all who are with you will be strong." 22 So they pitched a tent for Absalom on the top of the house, and Absalom went in to his father's concubines in the sight of all Israel. (2 Samuel 16:20-22)

No matter who counsels you, a foolish, greedy, an ambitious man or a wise man, what you *choose* to do, is on you. I know too many people who ask too many people the same question before they ever make a move. I'm sure the counsel varies, but the one asking is looking for the answer they like. Sometimes they are looking for a scapegoat, someone to blame if things go sideways.

The answer is in the Word of God. The counsel is in the Bible and our guidance is from Our Guide, the Holy Spirit.

Lust of the flesh, lust of the eyes, pride of life --- *whoredoms* and idolatry is never satisfied. It **cannot** be satisfied so it needs to be resisted and cast out.

For all that is in the world, the lust of the flesh, and the **lust of the eyes**, and the **pride of life**, is not of the Father, but is of the world. (John 2:16)

Absalom, daringly good looking, they say, was the son of David an adulterer, and Bathsheba an adulteress. So, what do you think that might make Absalom who saw his father with 8 wives and so many concubines. Eight wives--, come on man! So the urge to merge with David's concubines was the advice that Absalom would gladly take. Remember, Absalom had a brother that took it to a whole other level by raping his own half-sister. Solomon, Absalom's brother, had 700 wives and 300 concubines. *Whoredoms* ran deep in that bloodline.

The Children of Ammon

Wherefore hast thou despised the commandment of the Lord, to do evil in his sight? thou hast killed Uriah the Hittite with the sword, and hast taken his wife to be thy wife, and hast slain him with the sword of the children of Ammon.

Howbeit, because by this deed thou hast given great occasion to the enemies of the Lord to blaspheme, the child also that is born unto thee shall surely die. (2 Samuel 12:14)

The Ammonites were a very cruel people; evil had a stronghold in their bloodline. They sacrificed children.

David sent Uriah, an innocent man, out to battle to be killed by the Ammonites who were in constant skirmishes with the Israelites—kind of like a perpetual enemy.

We know the story of Uriah, so we know what happened in the physical realm. However, we don't know all of what happened in the spiritual realm. But we know that God is a God of balance, and we know the devil is a legalist. Uriah, an innocent man was sent back out to battle by his fake friend, David who was after Uriah's wife. On that battlefront, the soldiers who were called the *children of Ammon* shed Uriah's innocent blood.

This is occultic in that David *nominated* Uriah for death, unbeknownst to Uriah and most of the other people of the kingdom, and the Ammonites were essentially used to execute the innocent man.

Jesus came to Earth to be Husband to the Church. Jesus was and is innocent, while the church is supposed to be more beautiful than Bathsheba and certainly without spot, blemish, or wrinkle, but the Church is committing idolatry and adultery and other sins—with the devil and his evil representatives. The Jews turned Jesus over to the Romans for the Romans to kill Him—an innocent man. Like I said, *a scapegoat in case something goes wrong.* Jesus being crucified went terribly wrong for the devil, *did it not?* Can the Jews say, *"We didn't do it; the Romans did it?"*

God hates the *children* we create by demonic, occultic, and satanic **entanglements**. God hates the sin, but He still loves the sinner and gives us space and time to repent after the Word has come to us via the pastor, prophet, or by any other vessel. We should repent quickly. A broken heart and a contrite spirit He will not despise. So God is giving us time to get it together and repent, but the *children* of our sins, God will not abide. The *children* of our sins are the natural results of our own schemes and plots and plans to make ourselves look good, look successful—basically look uncursed, even though we may still need deliverance, even after salvation.

The *children* of our dark entanglements could be where the phrase, *Easy come, easy go* came from. Whatever we got from the dark kingdom, we don't really get to enjoy it. The blessings of the Lord make rich, and He adds no sorrow with it. Fake blessings from the dark kingdom have so much sorrow attached, and those coveted evil blessings do not come with the power to enjoy them--, like never. If so, only for a very short period of time. The "successful" criminal is always looking over his shoulder, he is paranoid, he is not relaxed and enjoying his wealth.

The children of demonic entanglements are demonic, look who their father is. They are demonic therefore they must be destroyed. This explains why eve very large gains by evil means don't last, either for the one who made the deal and certainly not for their natural children after they are deceased.

Whatever is gotten in the dark from the dark kingdom has strings galore and creates mega spiritual debt with it.

The children of Ammon were descendants of Ben-Ammi, the child produced by one of Lot's daughters sleeping with him after they got Lot drunk on two successive nights. Lot was Abraham's nephew. And Abraham was David's 10th great grandfather, or something like that. The Ammonites were forever feuding with the Israelites.

They were cousins, about 10 times removed, but still cousins.

The Ammonites were excessively cruel. They killed and ripped open pregnant women in battle. They seemed to have no limit to their meanness and evil. This would make sense because the Ammonites sacrificed children to the evil *god*, Molech. Adding to that, Lot's two daughters technically sacrificed themselves when they decided to get their father drunk and each have sex with him. (This adds a new meaning to the term, *Lot lizards*. Folks, I'm telling you, it is all in the Bible already.)

What can we expect, really? When Sodom and Gomorrah were destroyed, Lot's wife looked back when God told them NOT to look back, but she did and was turned into a pillar of salt. These two girls had a disobedient mother, and were raised in the presence of the *spirits* of Sodom and Gomorrah. Somehow the counsel they gained from the *spirits* in each of them was to commit incest. They also found it easy enough to get their own father drunk on two successive nights—so this may have been his habit. *Lot lizards*, like two creatures crawling all over their own father, Lot. How gross is this?

The children of Ammon were the hands that held the sword that killed Uriah in battle.

Read this carefully: **David wanted Uriah dead. Molech is the *god* that the Ammonites sacrifice to; Molech was their *god*.** **Molech did a favor for David—at least that was what David wanted in order to save face in front of his people. David may not have outwardly asked Molech, but David got something out of that evil idol *god*. DAVID NOW OWED MOLECH.**

God didn't kill Uriah. God wouldn't have killed Uriah. Molech's people killed Uriah.

Molech wants child sacrifice.

David has a brand new infant child. Molech wants that child.

Folks when you are out making your own side deals, your own devil deals, you've stepped out from under covering. What can God do for you when it goes a way that you don't think it should go? David fasted and prayed and went nearly crazy, but the child still died.

We serve a God of balance. David is in sin and God can't really help him, since God avenges all disobedience in our obedience. When we step into sin, who will help us? Who *can*? When you step into the dark kingdom, the kingdom of demons, devils, idols and false *gods* and you get *favors* from them, you **owe** them. Most of the tine you owe then generationally as far as they are concerned.

Favors from the evil kingdom are evil things; they are things that God does not condone and would never do. But in dark devil deals there are evil covenants. In those evil covenants are evil clauses and fine-fine print. You signed it, but did you read it first? You signed it in the spirit. You signed it with your own blood and the blood of your generations.

So did King David when he got Bathsheba and killed a man because of her pregnancy.

The Sword Shall Not Depart

God, still speaking through Nathan continued to tell David what else would befall him because of his sins.

Now therefore the sword shall never depart from thine house; because thou hast despised me, and hast taken the wife of Uriah the Hittite to be thy wife.

Thus saith the Lord, Behold, I will raise up evil against thee out of thine own house, and I will take thy wives before thine eyes, and give them unto thy neighbour, and he shall lie with thy wives in the sight of this sun.

For thou didst it secretly: but I will do this thing before all Israel, and before the sun. (2 Samuel 12:9-12)

That happened. What God said would happen, happened. Absalom slept with David's concubines on the advice of Ahithophel, in broad daylight for all to see. However, that didn't end well at all.

Absalom tried to overtake his own father to take over the kingdom. Absalom pursued David to kill him. The *spirit of Absalom* is a *takeover spirit*. God said that this *sword* would come from David's own house. Absalom's attempted takeover was not successful and Absalom ended up dead.

Another son. Gone.

But, David is still alive. Shouldn't a young man be able to *take* an old man? Consider again the words of the Prophet as the mouthpiece of the Lord:

> And David said unto Nathan, I have sinned against the Lord. And Nathan said unto David, The Lord also hath put away thy sin; **thou shalt not die.** (2 Samuel 12:13, *emphasis added, mine)*

Absalom wasn't privy to the conversation that the Prophet Nathan had with David, therefore he didn't know. God, showed His great love for David, after all was not David a man after God's own heart? In the midst of adultery and lies and murder, all of which is sin, and God hates sin. But God still loves the sinner. Folks, that's us. God is not a man that He should lie. God said to David, through the Prophet: **Thou shalt not die.**

Yes, David had sinned and sinned, but when the heart of God was made known to him, David repented quickly. God then gave him a Word, **Thou shalt not die.** Not only that, when David was a younger man and could have taken out the older King Saul, David spared Saul's life--, more than once. David respected the anointed of the Lord, King Saul. It seems that the Lord respects the anointing as well, even though Absalom didn't.

Absalom, your father King David had a Word from the Lord, surely you could never have done anything contrary to that Word. If you had prevailed, Absalom, that would have made God a liar, and **God is NOT a liar**. It is impossible for God to lie.

God did this so that, by two unchangeable things in which it is impossible for God to lie, we who have fled to take hold of the hope set before us may be greatly encouraged.
(Hebrews 5:18)

Man does not live by bread alone, but by every word that proceeds out of the mouth of God. David was actually alive and living by the Words that had proceeded out of God's mouth. Literally.

The Sins of the Ancestors

Saints of God, this is why in my prayers I repent for myself, my parents and my ancestors. Someone wrote me a note last week saying that it is too late to pray for ancestors:

I AM NOT TRYING TO PRAY ANCESTORS INTO HEAVEN, I AM PRAYING REGARDING BLOODLINE INIQUITY, asking the Lord to forgive it, in case no one in my family or bloodline has done that. That is why I repent for my parents and my ancestors, in the Name of Jesus. This is foundational work. I am praying regarding my foundation.

If you are *abiding* in Christ, you can boldly come to the Throne of Grace to receive Grace and Mercy in the time of trouble. But if you never ask God, if you feel you just can't ask Him. Feeling that what you are asking for is wrong or unholy – don't ask Him that. But if you are abiding in Christ, then ask. Your *abiding* requests need to be heard by God; ask Him. If you don't ask Him, you will get nothing, The Word says that we have not because we asked not.

Take a good look at your relationship with God. Do you want to be religious? Do you want to be religious like the Sadducees and the Pharisees, or do you want *relationship*? Pharisees and Sadducees probably thought they were so holy they didn't need to ask God for anything.

I will ask God. He said we can come boldly. Therefore, my *abiding* requests will be heard by God, Amen. I will ask Him for all things that I need for life and godliness, in the Name of Jesus.

I rather believe that I need to ask God for all things – even though there is *proviso* for it in the Word, that I am in Christ and walking upright before the Lord, not in sin, as much as it is possible for any human. I am agreeing with Heaven that I want that to come to me for my life and godliness, in the Name of Jesus, AMEN.

I am agreeing with the Word in order to pray my angels *through*. Even though God's answer to what I am asking Him for is YES and AMEN, I need those things to actually reach me. Therefore, I **agree** with the Word of God.

God has given me so much. Yet I will make my petitions known to Him. Praying and asking God to forgive my ancestors to remove the iniquity from my bloodline, through His Mercy, so I won't have to pay it is not an unreasonable request. He said ask anything.

Is Satisfaction Possible?

Is there something else? What else can I do for you today?

    Maybe the Lord is wanting to know if you **_can_** be satisfied. *Whoredoms and idolatry* are signs that a person is not and cannot be satisfied, if they are carrying those demons around. If they could be satisfied then they wouldn't be chasing everything they see, everything they think they want or see someone else with, like they've never had anything in their entire lives. If they could be satisfied, they wouldn't be jealous of other folks, their looks, their house, car, relationships, or bank accounts.

By the time David saw Bathsheba he already had 6 wives and 6 sons, David was married to Ahinoam, Abigail, Maacha, Haggith, Abital, and Eglah during his rule as king of Judah. Michal was his first wife, before the preceding list, but after Michal mocked David's worship, she was deemed barren and was sidelined as a queen consort. One source said that she did become pregnant but died in childbirth.

After David became king over both Judah and Israel, they moved from Hebron to the new capital, Jerusalem. There he saw Bathsheba. After all the sin and eventually marrying Bathsheba, David married another wife to make eight. Each of his first six wives bore David a son, while Bathsheba bore him four sons. One historian says that David had 20 children. Would that be enough wives and children to make a man *satisfied*?

So, why was his eye still roving? Why would any man still be looking and looking?

- *Whoredoms.*
- *Lust.*
- *Dissatisfaction.*
- *Greed.*
- *Pride.*

All the above are *spirits* you need to get rid of so God can bless you and you can get and **keep** your blessings. Even if you get blessed in some kind of way and you've got all those demons working in your life, they are going to find a way to get it from you. They come not but to steal, kill, and destroy. You will give it away. Throw it away. Showing it off. Somebody will take it –

Where Did Those Men Come From?

In the Book of Isaiah, Isaiah asked King Hezekiah, Who were those men and what did you show them in this palace?

Hezekiah responded, I showed them everything.

At that time Marduk-Baladan son of Baladan king of Babylon sent Hezekiah letters and a gift… Hezekiah received the envoys gladly and showed them what was in his storehouses—the silver, the gold, the spices, the fine olive oil—his entire armory and everything found among his treasures. There was nothing in his palace or in all his kingdom that Hezekiah did not show them.

Then Isaiah the prophet went to King Hezekiah and asked, "What did those men say, and where did they come from?"

"From a distant land," Hezekiah replied. "They came to me from Babylon."

The prophet asked, "What did they see in your palace?"

"They saw everything in my palace," Hezekiah said. "There is nothing among my treasures that I did not show them."

Then Isaiah said to Hezekiah, "Hear the word of the Lord Almighty: 6 The time will surely come when everything in your palace, and all that your predecessors have stored up until this day, will be carried off to Babylon. Nothing will be left, says the Lord.

Babylon doesn't have to send envoys in the natural; monitoring *spirits* show up in the spiritual realm and you may never know they are there. They are taking assessment of all you have and sometimes what you are going to have, how they can get it, take it, steal it from you.

Pride, the show off *spirit* will make a man show off in front of anyone who shows interest. They will put their successes and riches on display. Vanity will make a man pliable in the hands of anyone who sends him a gift or pays him a compliment. These two *spirits* are not becoming a king.

And what happened to Hezekiah? The Prophet Isaiah gave a Word from the Lord too. Prophets speak to kings; prophets have to be very bold and speak to power. So now that Hezekiah has put everything on display—for Babylon of all people, it will be captured and taken away from them, by Babylon.

When someone wants to know about your belongings, property, wealth and successes, consider who wants to know. Don't put all your business out in the streets and on social media.

Where did those spirits come from that make you take on their nature of greed, and lust, and all other works of the flesh?

Egypt? Babylon? The Dark Kingdom? Hell?

So stop telling them all your business.

Hezekiah is not so concerned. He says in Verse 8:

> "The word of the Lord you have spoken is good," Hezekiah replied. For he thought, "There will be peace and security in my lifetime." (Isaiah 39:8 NIV)

Just like in David's case, the bad thing that Hezekiah did didn't cause him to die, as a matter of fact his life had been extended by 15 years. Hezekiah was saying that whatever bad thing that would befall the people of the kingdom wouldn't affect him because he'd be gone by then.

Generational losses, heavy generational losses were prophesied by Isaiah, but Hezekiah was kind of flip and didn't seem to care. Sin causes personal loss and generational loss. In that sense you are a *king* for a lot of people. David was king and when he sinned it affected a lot of people. Hezekiah was king and when he sinned it affected also a lot of people. A good king cares; a good king avoids sin and wrongdoing. A selfish *spirit* in a king is unbecoming and does a lot of damage.

> When the righteous are in authority, the people rejoice: But when the wicked beareth rule, the people mourn. (Proverbs 29:2)

But back to David: How much is enough? How much wealth? How much fame? How much attention? For King David, how many wives is enough? How many women, David? So, I ask, if

David got delivered when the Word of the Lord came to him through Nathan? And if so, did he **stay** delivered?

> Now king David was old and stricken in years; and they covered him with clothes, but he gat no heat. (1 Kings) 1:1-2)

David was old and stricken in age and still worried about getting *"heat,"* so, they got him a young virgin, but he still got no heat. So, you tell me--, 8 wives and at least 10 sons, as many as 20 children, and he's still trying to get *heat*.

Come on *Zaddy*.

> Wherefore his servants said unto him, Let there be sought for my lord the king a young virgin: and let her stand before the king, and let her cherish him, and let her lie in thy bosom, that my lord the king may get heat. So they sought for a fair damsel throughout all the coasts of Israel, and found Abishag a Shunammite, and brought her to the king. And the damsel *was* very fair, and cherished the king, and ministered to him: but the king knew her not.

I don't know if for a man not getting an erection was the Old Testament way of saying, lights out or not, but it was serious enough that people had to intervene to help him out.

David died of natural causes at around 70 years old. Was he satisfied because he was satisfied, or was he just "heatless," the Bible doesn't really say. However, I like to think that a person who dies of natural causes means the person had some say so in when they would go on to Glory.

Me, Me, Me

But, like people, things, money, stuff – food --- if you are not satisfied then you will heap everything on your own lust. God will give you even **Such & Such** if you abide in Him and His Word abides in you, just ask, and it shall be given. He will give it to you.

However, some ask and do not receive…if certain criteria hasn't been met.

Ye ask, and receive not, because ye ask amiss, that ye may consume it upon your *lusts*.(James 4:3)

Until you get satisfied, or you are *satisfiable*, or you at least learn to behave yourself as if you have some home training, God may not be able to give you what you may be asking Him for. A lot of people like to say, God if you give me this, if you give me that, I will be a channel of blessing, that is what most people say they will do when God blesses them with abundance or prosperity.

If you want to be a channel of blessing, then you have to get <u>satisfied</u>,

You have to get all those raging, starving demons out of you that cannot be satisfied, such as *whoredoms, lust, greed, gluttony, alcoholism, seduction, pride, and I'm sure others*—any works of the flesh. They all come to steal, kill, and destroy. They can't be satisfied. So if they are in you they are making you act *like them* as you take on their nature then you will behave as an unsatisfied sort, yourself.

The more you yearn for, long for, and lust after things and stuff, the more these enemies of God will show up with the unspoken, *We can help you get all of that. We can help you get what you want.* If you say nothing to them, if you don't say, No! to them, then they come onboard. If you say nothing because you are spiritually unaware that this is happening, or you like these spirits and believe they will help you --, especially if you've become desperate, they will get into your life. If you don't resist them, they come onboard. If you don't resist them and get deliverance, they stay. That is how these *spirits* find humans that they call home.

They've gotta go, so God can bless you, because God is not going to bless those demons. Plus, they can't be satisfied, and they want you to have nothing. They are wasters, destroyers, swallowers, and emptiers. They will take everything from you until you have nothing again. Just that quick.

Why are you entertaining thieving, stealing demons in the first place? Oh, they are **your** demons, and you didn't think they'd steal from **you**?

Don't be deceived; they steal from everyone--, even you. And if they are near you, around you, or *in* your soul, they are definitely there to steal, kill and destroy. Else, they'd be somewhere else with the same agenda.

Why are you entertaining killing demons? They will turn on you in a New York minute.

Why are you entertaining destroying demons? Is it because you don't recognize them? You recognize them in others, but you can't see them in yourself, or in your own life?

How's your life lately? You must assess your life to see if stealing, killing, or destroying demons are involved in it. Are you well? Are you sick? Are you well off, or are you struggling, or broke? There is a spiritual reason behind everything that is happening in any life. If you sense the presence of evil spirits in your life, read the Word, pray, praise and worship, fast, and or take deliverance. They **must** go.

Until you get used to having things and being around prosperity, plenty, and abundance, then what is inside of you will cause you to consume whatever you receive on your own lust if you're not used to anything. They will make you go crazy spending, shopping, gifting, showing off. As they say, money burns holes in pockets.

Please consider this, the devil also has evil human agents that he wants to reward with stuff, things, money, prosperity – at least as bait to keep them on the hook doing evil for him in the Earth. It is the job of demons that think they live with you, to reroute your blessings to the evil human agents. Yeah, it's complex, isn't it? It is probably more complex than this, but I am sharing at the level that the Holy Spirit is allowing me to share right now.

Stones Into Bread?

Let's look at Jesus in the Wilderness temptation again:

The devil knew Jesus had fasted 40 days and Jesus was hungry, so the devil tried to tempt Him to change stones into bread. JESUS did not.

Yet, on at least two different occasions Jesus multiplied fishes and loaves to feed 4000 people on one account and 5000 people on another. The hungry man who is lusting for food – hungry for bread will not care what happens to other people; he won't care what happens to the multitude, he would have just taken the boy's lunch and eaten it himself. That is heaping on your own lust.

Not Jesus.

And when the tempter came to him, he said, If thou be the Son of God, command that these stones be made bread. But he answered and said, It is written, Man shall not live by bread alone, but by every word that proceedeth out of the mouth of God.
(Matthew 4:3-4)

I love this because Jesus is showing when He fed the Multitude, He was showing everybody, including the devil--, Hey, I CAN change this into food, I can change water into wine, I can multiply whatever is expedient for me to multiply, after I bless it; after I check with My Father.

Further, Jesus said: My meat is to do the will of Him who sent me. Jesus wasn't trying to entertain his flesh or stuff His face. Jesus didn't come here for that..

Jesus saith unto them, My meat is to do the will of him that sent me, and to finish his work. (John 4:34)

Life is more than meat, and the body is more than raiment. (Luke 12:23)

Jesus was not carnal or fleshly— He didn't come to Earth for His flesh, else He would have been feeding it and decorating it and entertaining it the whole time He was here.

Selah.

What Shall I Do?

Especially if God gives you this prosperity that many people keep asking Him for --- if it is for you to distribute to others you can't spend it on or hoard it up for yourself. You can't let lust, greed, pride or any of these other stealing, killing, destroying demons make you think you are keeping it for yourself, because you are really keeping it for **them**. You would be keeping it for the stealing, killing, and destroying *spirits* – to steal. They have ways, my friend, they are tricky and conniving.

And he spake a parable unto them, saying, The ground of a certain rich man brought forth plentifully:

And he thought within himself, saying, What shall I do, because I have no room where to bestow my fruits?

And he said, This will I do: I will pull down my barns, and build greater; and there will I bestow all my fruits and my goods.

And I will say to my soul, Soul, thou hast much goods laid up for many years; take thine ease, eat, drink, and be merry.

But God said unto him, Thou fool, this night thy soul shall be required of thee: then whose shall those things be, which thou hast provided?

So is he that layeth up treasure for himself, and is not rich toward God.
(Luke 12:16-21)

Having to work and toil is part of the Curse of the Law—we get redeemed from the Curse of the Law by Jesus Christ, not by uncursing ourselves by works of the flesh to make it look like we are out from under the Curse.

Just because a man looks blessed, doesn't mean he is blessed, fully delivered, and rich toward God.

In the preceding parable, the man with great abundance did not ask **GOD** what must he do with his newfound wealth. That man didn't seem to know that he was going to get this windfall, else he would already have been in conversation with God. That man didn't know the purpose of all this prosperity as he was so surprised by it.

That rich man decided within himself—he took counsel from the *spirits* that were within himself as to what he should do with this huge harvest. He went along with what his mind told him; he leaned on is own understanding.

The Bible doesn't say that he sought counsel, so who did he ask? God? Or, *not*-God? It would be better for any who are asking God for prosperity or wealth, or even *such and such* to ask God the purpose for this wealth, FIRST. Ask **before** receiving it, not just receiving it and then deciding what *you* want to do with it.

I talk about this more in my book, **The Spirit of Poverty**. The point is, unless we know why we are here and what we are supposed to be doing, both spiritually and in the natural, we don't even know how much money we need or the timing of that money to accomplish our assignment or assignments.

When the wisemen came and blessed Jesus they spread quite a bounty at the baby shower. Jesus had a lot of work to do. You could tell by the magnitude of His star that a King had come to Earth, and you bring kingly gifts to a King.

What about you? Jesus is King of kings and that makes you a little k king in the Earth. What is your budget for life and godliness like? Have you considered it at all? If you are not trying to find out what you are supposed to be doing kingdom-wise, then what do you need a budget for? Your flesh? To entertain and decorate your flesh?

Just like the guy who gets a big job fresh out of school—he's got disposable money, maybe enough to choke a horse. If he is not saved and, in the Kingdom, he has no idea what to do with it. He will either let his friends, family, or whatever spirits are hanging around him or *in* him decide how to spend it. Note, I didn't say what to do with it, I said how to spend it, because most people will be ready to spend it. They will be ready to go out and play. Galivant around the world and enjoy themselves. Travel, eat, entertain themselves.

That is, until they get used to having money. Until they get used to nice things, they won't try to acquire **every** nice thing; finally, those greedy eyes will become satisfied. His appetite may become satisfied. His travel lust may get under control. He may also learn to be satisfied with one woman instead of wanting every woman he sees, or imagines. This person will finally make themselves content with a few nice things. That's the unsaved guy, although he could get saved in this process.

So, you're saved, find out what your Purpose is and what you need to fulfill Destiny. That is a request God will gladly honor.

David Lost

But for now: Saints of GOD: Look at all David Lost by not being at war when he should have been at war. Of all that David lost, we know he lost at least three children. For your consideration, if he had been doing what he was supposed to have been doing instead of sinning, would the three children that he lost have been lost to him?

> And Nathan departed unto his house. And the Lord struck the child that Uriah's wife bare unto David, and it was very sick. (2 Samuel 12:15)

Saints of God: David's sin KILLED the firstborn of he and

Bathsheba. When you sin, you don't just sin for yourself, your children and sometimes your *children's* children will suffer because you wanted to party or play or sin.

But, go back to verse 13b: The Lord also hath put away thy sin; thou shalt not die. His Mercies fail not. If the Lord forgives you, you won't die – but iniquity is in the bloodline for the children and the grandchildren to suffer.

At the time of the rooftop scene, David already had children (and wives) that he could have been thinking or praying about. He could have been priesting for his family and praying for their wellbeing. He had affairs of state to deal with. Instead, he was gawking at Bathsheba bathing, on that rooftop.

There was, as of yet, no children between David and Bathsheba, so no child was in his mind at that time. Who are we kidding, David wasn't thinking about the kids he already had, why would having a new one change him? David was only thinking of himself and what David wanted. Did he think that Bathsheba wanted to sin against her husband, Uriah who was off at war? No, he was only selfishly thinking of himself. In times of war the men did not *go into* their wives. These women were not thinking they could get *busy* with their husbands, even if husbands were home on furlough.

It doesn't seem that Dvid was thinking about any of that. Just David.

God said through Nathan the Prophet, to David: You have done this secretly, but I will do what I'm going to do openly -- before the sun, as it is written in verses 11 and 12.

DAVID, even though God forgave the sin, and David didn't DIE – David LOST generationally.

Many of us may think that money and possessions as wealth – and it is. but people are wealth. Family which includes wives and children are wealth. Divine connections is WEALTH. Destiny helpers, friends, true friends, that's wealth. Prosperity is when you are moving in your spiritual gifts with Purpose and toward Destiny. Relationship with God is wealth; that is the true riches.

Don't let fresh sin, or old sin, unconfessed, unrepentant sin be the reason you lose wealth of any kind, especially relationship with God. Don't let sin be the reason you lose PEOPLE, especially family, especially a spouse or your children, relationships, or divine connections. David lost Uriah because of sin. Do we know who Uriah could have been to David after the war with the Ammonites was over? Uriah could have been a faithful bodyguard or armor bearer to David and could have quenched the Absalom debacle. But we don't know, do we? David never gave Uriah a chance to find out if he would have been loyal to him.

David lost. David lost a native son, a warrior citizen of that land.

David lost a natural son with Bathsheba because of sin and David's house became filled with turmoil because of his sin. David lost Absalom because of the curse that went along with the Bathsheba sin. The sword did not depart that house. David lost Amnon because after Amnon raped his own half-sister, Tamar, Absalom killed Amnon.

That was a bloody household just as the Lord has said through Nathan. By the time David's son, Solomon arrived David wanted to built a temple to the Lord, but God wouldn't allow it. He allowed Solomon because David had shed blood that was not sanctioned by

God. Not only Uriah, but that first child between David and Bathsheba was innocent blood that was shed.

When you should be AT WAR, be at WAR. When you should not be sinning, don't sin – but you protect what you have so far. by WARFARE. Had David been in the presence of the Lord instead of in the presence of Bathsheba he could have saved many of the lives that were lost. Of course, Solomon wouldn't have gotten here.

By the curse because of David's sin, the sword continued in that house. Solomon killed his own brother, Adonijah after David had died and Adonijah had tried to take the Throne.

When you are doing what GOD has instructed you to do that is when God will protect you and anything you have stewardship over and especially people that you have relationship with.

He will protect the relationships, themselves.

When you step out from under the covering of God, it's a free for all, at the hands of the devil and his evil human agents.

After Bathsheba became pregnant with the King's kid – the only thing David wanted to do was to protect his reputation in front of the people. Wives – he already had six, then seven with Bathsheba. Wives did as they were told back then, none of them would have left King David. But, David knew that if he lost the people, he would have lost the power.

It would have been better for David if he had thought of that before the sin, instead of the sin, instead of after – but anyhoo--,

David lost. He lost a lot, when he could have just asked GOD for anything, for everything–, even for *Such and Such* and God would have given it to Him. Any abiding request you make known to the Lord, He will answer, Yes, and AMEN.

> Now therefore the sword shall never depart from thine house; because thou hast despised me, and hast taken the wife of Uriah the Hittite to be thy wife.
>
> Thus saith the Lord, Behold, I will raise up evil against thee out of thine own house, and I will take thy wives before thine eyes, and give them unto thy neighbour, and he shall lie with thy wives in the sight of this sun.
>
> For thou didst it secretly: but I will do this thing before all Israel, and before the sun. (2 Samuel 12:10-12)

David LOST:

1. The sword will never depart from David's house—that's generational, folks. We are in Christ who is of the lineage of David – we have to fight. When

there is a season of war, we must fight and not be at ease in Zion.
2. God raised up evil against David from his own house – aren't we all now still having to fight household wickedness and household witchcraft?
3. Public shame for private sin. We all know that what is done in the dark will be brought to the light.

> For there is nothing covered, that shall not be revealed; neither hid, that shall not be known.Therefore whatsoever ye have spoken in darkness shall be heard in the light; and that which ye have spoken in the ear in closets shall be proclaimed upon the housetops. (Luke 12:2-3)

Prayer Section

1. Lord, in the Name of Jesus --Lord, have Mercy on me, a sinner. If I am none of Yours, give me a Godly sorrow and a repentant heart, and make me one of Yours, in the Name of Jesus.

2. I believe that Jesus is the Son of God and that He came to Earth of virgin birth. I believe that He was crucified and on the Third Day God raised Him from the dead and He now lives.

3. I believe in my heart, and I confess with my mouth that Jesus is Lord to the saving of souls, for the

redemption of mankind and to the Glory of God. Amen.

4. I cover myself with the Blood of Jesus.

5. Holy Ghost Fire, fall on these prayers, in the Name of Jesus.

6. Lord, forgive me for every selfish sin. Lord, forgive me for hidden sins. Lord, forgive me for secret sins, in the Name of Jesus.

7. Lord, forgive me for disobedience, rebellion, and ignorance, pride and greed. Forgive me for seeking things that I should not have even desired, and/or seeking them out of turn, or out of season, in the Name of Jesus.

8. Lord, forgive me for not being at war, or in war – or in spiritual warfare but instead at ease in Zion, in the Name of Jesus.

9. Lord, forgive me for every non-abiding, ungodly request that I have ever made of You, in the Name of Jesus.

10. Lord, forgive me for not accepting Your answer to me whether it was **No, Not now**, or **Not right now**, but instead chasing after my desired outcomes in the flesh and in league with the kingdom of darkness. Lord, forgive.

11. Lord, forgive me for every soulish and diabolical prayer that I have prayed that went to the second heaven, whether it was answered or not, and especially if it was answered and caused an evil covenant to be formed with the dark kingdom.

12. Lord, forgive.

13. I break that covenant now, in the Name of Jesus.

14. LORD, You said in your Word that your people shall never be ashamed, LORD do not bring me to shame for seeking that which I should never have even looked at or ran after, in the Name of Jesus.

15. Lord, especially forgive me if I took from the least of Yours, from the least of these--, Lord have Mercy and show me a way to restore or make it right against anyone that I have oppressed or stolen from. Lord, let me make it right again, in the Name of Jesus.

16. Lord, forgive me for all sexual sin of every kind, in the Name of Jesus.

17. Lord, forgive me for breaking any Godly covenant, whatsoever, in the Name of Jesus.

18. Father, forgive me for interfering in anyone's covenant, especially a

marriage covenant, whether I was aware of it at the time, or not, in the Name of Jesus.

19. Lord, regarding my marriage, please release me from all iniquity, blot out the iniquity of interfering in anyone else's marriage – EVER, in the Name of Jesus.

20. Lord, forgive me for bloodshed, for shedding the blood of the innocent, in the Name of Jesus.

21. SON OF DAVID, have Mercy.

22. Son of David have Mercy on me.

23. Son of David have Mercy. LORD, have Mercy on me and let the SWORD depart from my house, in the Name of Jesus.(X2)

24. LORD have Mercy and do not allow evil, whether household or other evil

be raised up to have its way against me, in Jesus' Name.

25. LORD protect my house, my marriage, my children, my family, in the Name of Jesus.

26. LORD forgive me for not asking YOU for everything that I need for life and for godliness, even SUCH and SUCH, in the Name of Jesus.

27. Lord, I bind and paralyze every power, *spirit*, and evil covenant working against me, against my receiving everything, every blessing you have for me, because I know Your answer to my abiding prayers are YES and AMEN.

28. Lord, deliver me. Deliver me –, YES from things that are oppressing me, in the Name of Jesus.

29. LORD, BY YOUR SPIRIT, DELIVER ME FROM THINGS I AM DOING THAT OPPRESS OTHERS, IN THE NAME OF JESUS. (x3)

30. Lord, deliver ME FROM WAYS THAT I HAVE, FROM ATTITUDES THAT I CARRIY AND NURTURE THAT OPPRESS OTHERS, IN THE NAME of Jesus.

31. Son of David, have Mercy on me.

32. Son of David, have Mercy on me, and deliver me, in the Name of Jesus.

33. I seal these declarations, decrees, prayers and words across every dimension, realm, era, age, and timeline, past, present, and future, to infinity by the Blood of the Lamb and the Holy Spirit of Promise.

34. Any retaliation against these prayers, decrees, words, declarations on the speaker, the pray-er, or anyone who hears these words, or will ever pray them, backfire on the sender to infinity and without Mercy, in the Name of Jesus.

35. Lord, I thank You, and I count this as done, in the Name of Jesus.

AMEN.

Dear Reader:

Thank you for acquiring and reading this book. I pray it has liberated your thinking and that the Word of the Lord has brought deliverance wherever you may have needed deliverance.

Pray the prayers so the curses that came upon the House of David do not manifest in your house, your life, your marriage, or in your children, in the Name of Jesus. Amen

Shalom,

Dr. Marlene Miles

Prayerbooks by this author

While most books by this author have prayer points either throughout the book or at the end, there are some books that are only prayers. You just open up the book and pray. They are listed below:

Prayers Against Barrenness: *For Success in Business and Life*

Fruit of the Womb: *Prayers Against Barrenness*

Beauty Curses, *Warfare Prayers Against*
https://a.co/d/5Xlc2OM

Courts of Marriage: Prayers for Marriage in the Courts of Heaven
(prayerbook) https://a.co/d/cNAdgAq

Courtroom Warfare @ Midnight
(prayerbook) https://a.co/d/5fc7Qdp

Demonic Cobwebs *(prayerbook)*
https://a.co/d/fp9Oa2H

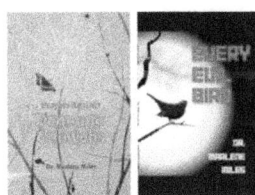

Every Evil Bird https://a.co/d/hF1kh1O

Gates of Thanksgiving

Spirits of Death, Hell & the Grave, Pass Over Me and My House

Throne of Grace: Courtroom Prayer

Warfare Prayer Against Poverty
https://a.co/d/bZ611Yu

Other books by this author

AK: The Adventures of the Agape Kid

Already Married in the Spirit: *Why You May Not Be Married in the Natural*

AMONG SOME THIEVES

Ancestral Powers

Anti-Marriage, *The Spirit of*

Backstabbers https://a.co/d/gi8iBxf

Barrenness, *Prayers Against*
https://a.co/d/feUltIs

Battlefield of Marriage, *The*

Blindsided: *Has the Old Man Bewitched You?* https://a.co/d/5O2fLLR

Break Free from Collective Captivity

Casting Down Imaginations

Churchzilla, The Wanna-Be, Supposed-to-be Bride of Christ

Curses of Blind Men

Demonic Cobwebs (prayerbook)

Demonic Time Bombs

Demons Hate Questions

Devil Loves Trauma, *The*

Devil Weapons: Unforgiveness, Bitterness,...

The Devourers: Thieves of Darkness 2

Do Not Swear by the Moon

Don't Refuse Me, Lord (4 book series)
https://a.co/d/idP34LG

Dream Defilement

The Emptiers: *Thieves of Darkness, 1*
https://a.co/d/5I4n5mc

Evil Touch

Failed Assignment

Fantasy Spirit Spouse
https://a.co/d/hW7oYbX

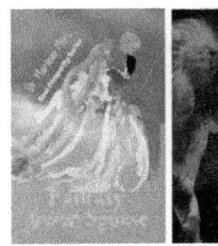

FAT Demons (The): *Breaking Demonic Curses*

The Fold (5-book series)

- The Fold (Book 1)
- Name Your Seed (Book 2)
- The Poor Attitudes of Money (3)
- Do Not Orphan Your Seed (4)
- For the Sake of the Gospel (5)
- My Sowing Journal

Gang Ups: Touch Not God's Anointed

got HEALING? Verses for Life

got LOVE? Verses for Life

got HOPE? Verses for Life

got money? https://a.co/d/g2av41N

How to Dental Assist

How to Dental Assist2: Be Productive, Not Wasteful

I Take It Back

Legacy

Let Me Have A Dollar's Worth https://a.co/d/h8F8XgE

Level the Playing Field

Living for the NOW of God

Lose My Location https://a.co/d/crD6mV9

Man Safari, *The*

Marriage Ed. Rules of Engagement & Marriage

Made Perfect in Love

Money Hunters: Beware of Those

Money on the Altar https://a.co/d/4EqJ2Nr

Mulberry Tree https://a.co/d/9nR9rRb

Motherboard (The) - *Soul Prosperity Series*

Name Your Seed

Occupy: *Until I Return*

Plantation Souls

Players Gonna Play

Power Money: Nine Times the Tithe

https://a.co/d/gRt41gy

The Power of Wealth *(forthcoming)*

Powers Above

The Robe, Part 1, The Lessons of Joseph

The Robe, Part II, The Lessons of Joseph

Seasons of Grief

Seasons of Waiting

Seasons of War

Second Marriage, Third--, *Any Marriage*

https://a.co/d/6m6GN4N

Sift You Like Wheat

Six Men Short: What Has Happened to all the Men?

Soul Prosperity soul prosperity series 3

https://a.co/d/5p8YvCN

Souls Captivity soul prosperity series 2

The Spirit of Anti-Marriage

The Spirit of Poverty

StarStruck

Such & Such: You Could Have Just Asked Me

SUNBLOCK

The Swallowers: *Thieves of Darkness,* 3

Take It Back

This Is NOT That: How to Keep Demons from Coming at You

Time Is of the Essence

Too Many Wives: *Why You Have Lady Problems*

Tormenting Spirits
https://a.co/d/dAogEJf

Toxic Souls

Triangular Power *(series)*

- Powers Above
- SUNBLOCK
- Do Not Swear by the Moon
- STARSTRUCK

Uncontested Doom

Unguarded Hours, *The*

Unseen Life, *The* (forthcoming)

Upgrade: How to Get Out of Survival Mode

- Toxic Souls (Book 2 of series)
- Legacy (Book 3 of series)

The Wasters: *Thieves of Darkness*, Bk 2
https://a.co/d/bUvI9Jo

What Have You to Declare? What Do You Have With You from Where You've Been?

When I Was A Child, *I Prayed As a Child*

When the Devourer is Rebuked

https://a.co/d/1HVv8oq

The Wilderness Romance *(series)* This series is about conducting a Godly relationship and marriage with someone who is a Wilderness person. It is about how to recognize it and navigate through it. These books are about how not to get caught up in such.

- *The Social Wilderness*
- *The Sexual Wilderness*
- *The Spiritual Wilderness*

Other Series

The Fold (a series on Godly finances)
https://a.co/d/4hz3unj

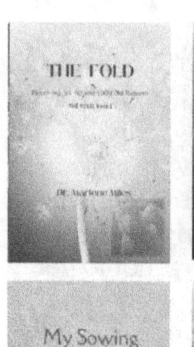

Soul Prosperity Series https://a.co/d/bz2M42q

Spirit Spouse books

https://a.co/d/9VehDSo

https://a.co/d/97sKOwm

Thieves of Darkness series

Triangular Powers https://a.co/d/aUCjAWC

Upgrade (series) *How to Get Out of Survival Mode* https://a.co/d/aTERhX0

Notes:

www.ingramcontent.com/pod-product-compliance
Lightning Source LLC
LaVergne TN
LVHW022323080426
835508LV00041B/2176